The
Bird-while

MADE IN MICHIGAN SERIES

GENERAL EDITORS

Michael Delp
Interlochen Center for the Arts

M. L. Liebler
Wayne State University

ADVISORY EDITORS

Melba Joyce Boyd
Wayne State University

Stuart Dybek
Western Michigan University

Kathleen Glynn

Jerry Herron
Wayne State University

Laura Kasischke
University of Michigan

Thomas Lynch

Frank Rashid
Marygrove College

Doug Stanton

Keith Taylor
University of Michigan

A complete listing of the books in this series can be found online at wsupress.wayne.edu

The Bird-while

POEMS BY KEITH TAYLOR
WITH ILLUSTRATIONS BY TOM POHRT

WAYNE STATE UNIVERSITY PRESS
DETROIT

Library of Congress Control Number: 2016952986
ISBN 978-0-8143-4240-4 (paperback)
ISBN 978-0-8143-4241-1 (ebook)

∞

Publication of this book was made possible by a generous gift from the Meijer Foundation. Additional support provided by the Michigan Council for Arts and Cultural Affairs and the National Endowment for the Arts.

DESIGNED BY LIBBY BOGNER, GOOD DONE DAILY
TYPESET BY RACHEL ROSS
COMPOSED IN MRS EAVES

Wayne State University Press
Leonard N. Simons Building
4809 Woodward Avenue
Detroit, Michigan 48201-1309

Visit us online at wsupress.wayne.edu

For all those who have lingered with me
in the bird-while–
Christine and Faith, of course,
but also, and in particular,
Dale Hutchinson, Dan Minock, and Macklin Smith.

CONTENTS

A Bird-while. In a natural chronometer, a Bird-while may be admitted as one
of the metres, since the space most of the wild birds will allow you to make your
observations on them when they alight near you in the woods, is a pretty
equal and familiar measure.

Emerson's Journal, May 14, 1838

PICASSO AND THE TAJ MAHAL

My house is a labyrinth
of unexplored corridors
leading off to Taj Mahals
that rise out of the mist at dawn.

My house contains mountains
and rivers and crimson sunbirds
using their forked tongues to collect
pollen from flowers that don't grow
anywhere close to here.

There's a place in the basement of my house
where all the lines of time
intersect and where I stand for whole moments
alone on a street in Paris
before a small gallery—1971,
and Picasso is still alive!

THE COLLECTIONS IN LONDON

1.

In a Cabinet of Curiosities

hidden in the British Museum—
yes, in a dark and dusty corner,
two shelves up from the floor—a merman,
brown, mummified, less than two feet long,
holds his skeletal hands to his head
and grimaces. He's been drying there
for two hundred and fifty years now.
The scales on his tail are flaking off.

2.

The Cattle on the Parthenon's South Frieze

would have been like the motherless calf
that chose my father as a parent,
following him everywhere—at chores,
or picking rhubarb from the garden,
that even wanted to follow him
to school, using her wet nose to nudge
the boy, who soon wished there were some god
close-by, hungry for a sacrifice.

B A N F F : Running Away

I was young enough to believe that when moments felt significant
they probably were. I saw sacraments everywhere

       so knee-deep in snow
       behind the picnic shelter
       where I went to take a leak
       I looked up
       at mountains only
       partially cloud shrouded

and was sure that this must mean something. But metaphor wasn't
imminent, or it was hiding just past the edge of my loneliness.

HITCHHIKING AND IMMORTALITY

I was not paying much attention
in those days but still recognized it
immediately: nightingale song—
full-throated and resonant drifting
out of the woods beside a highway
somewhere in central France, where no cars
slowed in scintillating evening light
and where I thought I might never die.

AT THE FLOWER MERCHANT'S IN TOULOUSE

Basques and Spaniards, French peasants
not a generation removed from dirt floors
and speaking the old language of the South

yell at each other in the warehouse
beside the railroad tracks
where the flower wholesaler won't give me work

among all the red and yellow blossoms
brought north through the night
that must get cut

then wrapped before they wilt
and where the scents rise in a mix strong enough
to turn the whole place quiet.

SOUTH OF TOULOUSE: Snow

The inn was next to the stables where I lived above the clubhouse. They paid me four francs an hour, plus meals, to wash dishes and sweep floors. In January there was one cold day that actually felt like winter, and I watched a feeble snowfall through the window above the sink.

> I jumped
>   over the gate after work
> and snow fluffed
>   away like dust
> when I landed
>   on the horse path.

I left clear footprints surrounded by thin snow that melted in just a few minutes.

THE CRITICISM OF MY FRENCH POEMS

Our relationship was probably
over by then, but I let her read
the only copies—each clean and short
with simple, fragile lines. She walked past
a window, reached out, and dropped them all.
I saw poems fluttering onto streets
or into those clipped Parisian trees.
Some caught a breeze, floating up, away.

MY DAUGHTER'S NARCOLEPSY

Before we received the official
diagnosis, we loved to recount
her sleep episodes. My favorite:
the Louvre, in front of those gigantic
paintings David made celebrating
the coronation of Josephine
and Napoleon before the French
nobles. My daughter drooled on the bench.

WHEN THE GIRLS ARRIVED IN COPENHAGEN

and left the station, near midnight,
snow fell in soft piles on their hats
and backpacks.

No cars or people passed
while they walked
down the hushed streets.

Through windows without blinds or curtains
they could see Danes bathed in blue
television light

or quietly reading in uncluttered rooms
small novels perhaps about two girls
long ago walking through snow.

AFTER SHE WAS SICK

on the way to Calcutta,
she sat by an open door
sucking in the thick monsoon
air. Outside the train, the night
was a moist black wall broken
only occasionally
by light from a village fire.

BHARATPUR: Dying Antelope

The nilgai   blue bull
close enough to cow
mother of us all
to be holy

is dying in a copse beside the road to the lodge. No one dares euthanize it.
Every morning the jackals and striped hyenas have moved closer, but they, too,
seem governed by the prohibitions and wait for the nilgai to die.

At night their hungry howls
like surprised cries
from children in pain
startle our windows.

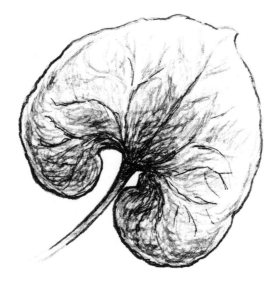

A RETURN

When she bent over the twins
who were sleeping on the floor,
I thought that the sadness
and wisdom of her trip
still clung to her and hoped
for the time that would arrive
soon enough when she could be silly
again, loveably ordinary,
and I could look at her unafraid.

MAPPING THE RIVER

1.

A Beginning

Headwaters here don't spring up. They seep
out between horizons of gravel
and clay. Black soil glistens more like slime
than dirt before the improbable
silent drop into the first puddle.
A hint of current almost hidden
beneath the long grasses. Not a stream
yet but a suggestion of river.

2.

Green Light

. . .

just during a few weeks, full summer
into September, on quiet days,
warm, humid but not hot—and the light
above the river turns green, like leaves,
reeds, water weeds or water itself
on its gently inexorable
slide through hills to the blue lakes beyond.

3.

On the Elimination of Dams

We want them down and water running
freely past the remnants of old mills
or small abandoned parts plants that made
cigar lighters for black Model Ts.

And yet . . . those perfect lonely moments
when we want only to watch the fall
of water, to feel the spray, to hear—
thankfully—only the dam's white noise . . .

4.

A State-Threatened Species

for Sara Alderstein-Gonzalez

The wavy-rayed lampmussel, yellow
or almost green, needs the small-mouthed bass
to host its young. Females siphon sperm
floating randomly in the river,
then lure the fish with a fake minnow,
squirting fertilized eggs into gills.
In a month the juveniles fall off
into sand. They try to start again.

5.

At the Mouth

After the bridge on West Jefferson
and a cheap marina on the bank
opposite the DNR boat launch,
the river opens to swamps dotted
with white egrets and great blue herons,
water trickling slowly over muck,
toward the last green barrier island
that shields us from a dark horizon.

6.

Dead Man's Point

They use another name for it now,
that cold place where the Huron empties
into Lake Erie, where the Detroit
used to bring bodies down from the north.
The dead would hang up in the rushes
or on the gray-brown log snags, often
disappearing under snow and ice,
their bones scattered and gone by breakup.

STONE TOOLS

after John M. O'Shea

Three thousand years ago someone stopped
on a small hill, unnoticed now
behind a postwar subdivision
but only a block up from the river.

He sat on a large rock, a glacial
erratic, for an afternoon and chipped
a stone point from a piece of chert.

He left his sharp-edged flakes scattered
and glistening under the oak leaves.

THE DAY THE TREES CAME DOWN

we weren't home so only imagine
the wind, its microburst slamming
straight down for ten brutal seconds,
the cracks as three oaks uprooted,
falling like a giant's pick-up sticks,
a puzzle or clutter across the yard.

One split the house next door,
just missing the articulate young nurse
who lived in the apartment upstairs.

I thought they would outlast me.

Maybe it was just our turn for ten seconds
of bad luck, for the $7000 bill.
There's no insurance that covers this.

CIRCLE IN THE WIND

until the wind turns
from the west

spring and promise
of new petals

of a breeze ruffling
the hairs on my arm

_____

yet gusts
rip old leaves

through our bed
of hyacinths

_____

there can be a dance
in the wind

at water's edge

chaos of hair blowing—
a choreography

gone in a whisper
a puff

of beauty blown off
leaving a scent

an impression
the feel of something held

_____

a hand chisels
letters into the wind

as it softens
and slows

———

when the land is hot
beneath the south wind

the whirlwind speaks

dust devils dance
across the dry prairie

and lightning cracks
an early evening sky

———

leaves and seeds
fall and are blown

into new
more fertile countries

an unlucky wind
from the east

low pressure rising
the world spins

———

winged old man
down from the north

white beard blowing
in a devouring wind

———

we would harness
these stallions of wind

beg them
to help us

heal the world
we damaged

———————

dry wind cuts
cheek and forehead

snow slithers
like wispy snakes

from roofs
across roads

until the wind turns
from the west

SEA AND RAIN: Lake Michigan

after James McNeill Whistler, 1865

There is a dance at water's edge,
a movement between the lake, its sand,
and the horizon where lake becomes cloud.

Between those lines our world's
a thin wash of muted tones, beige
and gray with a hint of white,

almost abstract, until the dancer
steps out into the pool.
She makes the whole thing real.

READING LATE

Patina of sweat along her arms—
she runs beside the lake, past the glow
of lights from my study, a whisper
like cicada calls in hazy air,
uncertain, grating on late summer
nights, not memory, barely desired
among piles of other people's words,
noiseless waves breaking against her feet.

CHASING THE ANCIENT MURRELET

Ancient . . . because of a gray mantel
                              thrown over its shoulders,
                    which look hunched against the weather

of the North Pacific, its real home,
                              too far from this place
                    at the edge of Lake Michigan

to be imagined, where the untouched
                              but beautiful young
                    run down the beach in summertime

longing to leave their parents, who make
                              steel appliances
                    and claim to love the wind and winter.

The bird is lost or brave or blown here
                              by westerlies strong
                    enough to reshape its instincts,

to bring it down to the dirty mouth
                              of a river that drains
                    the abandoned car factories

of South Bend, and the ancient murrelet
                              bobs in these choppy
                    irregular freshwater swells,

diving, often, after crustaceans
                              that haven't lived here
                    for a geologic epoch,

but taking what minnows it can find
                    to keep hunger off
        until it dies, here, in a place

it doesn't belong, where it can't find
                    the right food or mate,
        but where I find it, following

clear directions on the internet,
                    to catch a quick glimpse—
        as it rises between waves—

of its two-toned bill, and the large head—
                    bulky, oversized
        on its small diminished body.

CASTLE, NOWHERE

—Constance Fenimore Woolson

Satellites have plotted
every wave that plays
across the surface of the largest lakes.
Sonar and submersibles
have mapped every centimeter and shipwreck.

I won't *come out one evening*
unexpectedly upon a shore
with *water stretching away*
grayly in the fog-veiled moonlight,
won't hear *the dip of light oars*
somewhere out in the gray mist,

a rhythm I could follow
to ship or castle or a cabin
on an island lush with thimbleberry,
low-bush blueberry,
wild strawberries, and an apple tree,
a few trout in streams that never freeze,
some books, enough timber so I could
glean downed wood all through winter,

a place sketched in the corner
of a rain-soaked page
in an explorer's notebook, centuries back,
just that once, and then forgotten.

ONE SPECIES TO MOURN

—Aldo Leopold

1.

Some mounted specimens still
have a luminescent sheen
on their rusty breast feathers.
Fewer, males mostly, have traces
of their glistening blue backs—

we called them "blue meteors" here
when we could pick one from a flock
and watch it flutter into roost
below the dark-green canopy
of a beech or oak forest.

The glass eyes of the stuffed birds,
brown or red or made from sparkling buttons,
reflect us back to ourselves.
The unmounted birds in specimen cases
have threads of cotton batting
wriggling from empty eyeholes.

Most of the feet on the museum birds
must be wrong, more like broken sticks
than toes that could grab
a branch or twig beside their squabs,
the one chick each year they could
invest against their tenuous future.
They fed their young the protein-rich
lining of their stomach wall,
white and known as "pigeon milk."

2.

At twilight you shall eat flesh,
and in the morning you shall
be filled with bread . . .
Exodus 16:12

When I shoot my rifle clean
   To pigeons in the skies,
I'll bid farewell to pork and beans,
   And live on good pot pies.
Niles Republican, *May 6, 1843*

We never knew when they were coming
but we usually needed them—
unlimited protein
falling from the sky;
god's bounty;
big bread.

Then came the telegraph.
Then came the train.

3.

We were good at slaughter
and remembering slaughter:

knock one from its roost,
blind it, clip its wings,

use an old piece of burlap string
to tie its leg to a log.

Scatter some beech nuts
and wait.

The bird will flutter then hop up
on the stool we made for it.

More birds will come and once
they're all feeding, drop the net.

You can get 600 at one time!
Then crush their heads.

4.

We don't have the data
to remember the living birds—
just a few rough counts:

Audubon's flock for three days and nights
blocking out the sun and stars,
wheeling and twisting
within their continued lines,
which then resembled
the coils of a gigantic serpent.

A quiet old man in Spring Lake
tried to remember the flocks
he'd seen sixty years earlier,
great consecutive arcs of birds
against a yellowing late-summer sky,
flying above fields, the wheat
cut and piled into stooks
awaiting the threshing crews.
He built a house where he could
paint giant canvases,
appropriate to his subject.

His neighbors called him eccentric.
His paintings are forgotten.

5.

just passing by

Ectopistes migratorius

passengers here, with us

(after Joel Greenberg)

THE LAST ROOST

There's a record written years later:
up in Emmet County, after months
of slaughter—50,000 a day
sent to Chicago—the passenger
pigeons rose in their last flock, circled
over Lake Michigan, terrified
of land, and finally exhausted
rested, relieved perhaps, in water.

DRUMMOND ISLAND FOSSILS

Take the ferry east out of Detour
then drive up across the alvar plains
to a path that leads you to the shore.
There, rock ledges step down to the lake.
Kneel. Look closely. You'll see shadows, then
limestone honeycombed with delicate
coral branches that waved from the floor
of an ocean we can't imagine.

STATUE OF THE BLIND GIRL

Nydia, the blind flower girl of Pompeii after
Edward Bulwer-Lytton and Randolph Rogers

She listens, not to the green world exploding
around her, not to Vesuvius howling—

the hour has come; of two working in the field
one shall be taken; of two women grinding wheat
one shall be taken; Vesuvius erupts
and the black clouds descend; now we know
this is the hour when the thief will come—

she listens, not to the temples collapsing
or the birds crying from shriveled gardens,

she listens for the one voice who must call,
the one who knows, now that the hour has come,
that she can take us to the boats

and she suffers with our trembling earth,
gagging like the rest of us in this closed air,

but when we walk around her,
to the shadowed side, closer to the wall,
we can see the hidden profile,

the one that disguises her joy

now that the hour has come,
the one that shows her smile.

PRAIRIE FIRE

i.m.: Donald Taylor

Uncertain about the difference
between his memory and the myth,
the thing he'd been told and what he'd seen,
he kept the image of rising clouds
of black smoke looming like dark mountains
to the west, with a flickering skirt
of fire growing larger, noisier,
dancing through the grass toward home.

NO ONE DARED CALL IT BEAUTIFUL

(the Duck Lake Fire)

1.

No one died
but we paddled
quietly through the burn.
We avoided the snags, charred
even in midstream. Tag alders
and sedges already sprouted on the banks.

Some slopes and dune edges
were nothing but ash. They fluffed
away when we landed.
They crackled underfoot.

2.

Summer homes and businesses lost
in a May fire, then salvage logging
takes the larger dead trees for pulpwood.
Still, only a month later, I walk
through green patches of fresh bracken fern
under the black sticks that were jack pines.
Millions of cones, exploded open
and seedless, float down the Two Hearted.

LATER

A year after the Sleeper Lake Fire,
jack pine seedlings push up through the peat
that didn't burn off late last August.
They grow an inch high around the edge
of a swamp covered in new rushes,
emerald green against the charred trees,
dead except for their cones forced open
by heat, scattering seeds in the wind.

I WILL LIFT UP MINE EYES

When the world is finally theirs again,
they will come down from the hills
out west of town.
They'll follow straight lines—
they learn so quickly!—even using the bridges
that haven't yet crumbled
into walls or into nothing at all.

When they stop to hunt rats
or raccoons at a house
broken open when oaks blew over,
they'll step gingerly—they are always
so careful where they place their paws—
on what's left of our moldy books,
avoiding the still shimmering plastic
shards of the Anthropocene.

LANDSCAPE OF FEAR

Fear belongs to man, not to the world
—Mary Ruefle

The valley or slope or streambed
lies in just the one way

that everything moving across it—
rodent
or migrating herds of ungulates—

could be measured
by an eye
that's hidden above
under some camouflaged overhanging ledge.

The beasts that would be prey
understand:

they avoid this landscape
for generations, centuries,

and plants that elsewhere
are eaten down to the root

grow here,
lush and extravagant.

The land itself changes.

IN THE PRESENCE OF LARGE PREDATORS

We're sure now: wolves have found their way back
here, to the Lower Peninsula,

first reported by a park ranger
looking north across the Straits, through snow,
uncertainly watching a gray pair
skitter across the ice, their tracks lost

in the storm, then only a few prints
for years, some scat found twenty miles south,

before a night vision camera
catches movement, and the lanky legs,
massive chest, and triangular head,
those green eyes glowing once again

here, enter the frame, and even though
we've learned our lessons and fear there are
many reasons not to celebrate
anything without reservation,

we listen expectantly, with hope,
for the quiet yip of pups hiding
close to an overgrown two-track road

or look off across the lake, peering
through fog at the far shore to a woods
suddenly transformed into forest,
alive again under fragile light.

Addendum: After the DNA

OK. So they're coyotes.
Or only the mother
was a wolf.

We have nothing
to worry about.

SIGN

After long walks down sandy power-line cuts
looking
for wolf tracks

I hear
of a pile of scat on a trail to the bog
and find

turd-shaped clumps of deer fur
filled
with ragged pieces of bone.

THE HYBRID AT BURT LAKE

i.m.: Tom Andrews

The straight line of prints looks planned
as it moves down the thin strip
of sand at the wild north end
of Burt Lake. Here,
far from docks and summer homes, the hybrid
stalked a goose weakened by molt,
ripped out the fleshy breast meat
and left the rest to a cloak
of green and purple flies.

Above the wash of waves against the beach,
we hear a creature shuffle off
into the forest behind us—
a bird, perhaps a squirrel, maybe something bigger.
We will never know for sure.

ALL I'M TRYING TO DO

Still enough of a farm boy to stop
when I see a calf bawling outside
a barbed-wire fence, its mother, sad-eyed,
resigned, snuggling up to the tines,
ruminating—I try to lift it
over the fence, away from coyotes
or the wolves, returned to our forests
now, who have surely heard this newborn
squealing, but it kicks out at my head
though all I'm trying to do is help.

AFTER GOYA'S DREAM

for Nicholas Delbanco

Have we become too comfortable
with those creatures rising from the night,
half-men flying in from the forest?
Have we celebrated their weirdness
and domesticated their terror?
Did we invent the beneficence
of owls, desire too desperately
the protection of the bright-eyed lynx?

BANFF : Running Away, Ducks

If it happened now, I would know what the ducks were and might make a
reasonable guess about why they had stayed so long into winter, swimming
in the one bit of open water a couple of hundred yards above Bow Falls. The
river's fast and noisy there, even when its surface is frozen.

Two brown ducks, small, round, drifting down
until blocked by ice, then climbing out
to fly back to the top of open water.

The current pushes them downstream again
until one slips under. It never comes up.

BIRD RESCUE

for Sherri Smith

Some reasonable people think
the horned grebe floating
down the Detroit River
between car-sized ice floes—
diving deep into current
to search for fish,
then rising into a pool
of oil or synthetic fuel—
deserved to die: maladjusted,
they say, to our new world.
But the grebe gasped its way
to shore ice, water
seeping through spoiled feathers.

A sentimental soul found
it there, quivering in snow,
tried to wipe away the oil,
then brought it here. We warmed
the bird, fed it mealworms,
and waited for some liveliness
before bringing out our Dawn,
detergent of choice for bird rescue.

I stared into its red eye
and held the grebe, trembling
and tense, under a gentle stream
of water warmer than anything
it had felt in months,
while the real bird rescuer
worked the soap in, lifting
the oil out—she succeeded
when the feathers fluffed
on their own. The grebe was light

in my hands. Its hollow bones
felt delicate, breakable,
until a wing flapped against me,
strong and longing for flight.

A day later we took
our horned grebe down
to the Huron and the one patch
of open water below Barton Dam.
It scuttled out of its cage,
dove quickly, then surfaced
a few yards farther away,
ruffled its feathers, and drifted
down to join the indifferent ducks.

THE WEAVER

Now that her eyes are failing, the weaver
visits an abandoned gravel pit
in early May just when bank swallows
have returned to dig
their burrows into the loose cliffs.
She takes an old pillow,
fraying, about to split,
filled with the white down
of domesticated geese. She stands
at the lip of the pit,
rips open the pillow,
and releases handfuls of white feathers
into the drafts blowing up
against her. The swallows
swirl in, pluck feathers
from the air, swoop close to pick
the small ones that catch
in the weaver's hair.

A RUBY-THROATED HUMMINGBIRD TRIPTYCH

1. If You Want to Find a Nest
for Dave Ewert

lie down on a long-abandoned road
in a northern forest—a warm day,
with just a few insects—and look up.
With luck you might see a hummingbird
stopping between dead twigs of red pine
collecting shimmering gossamer
from spiders. With more luck you might see
her carry it off to line her nest.

2. Data from a Late-Summer Garden

Great spangled fritillary working
the butterfly bush, long tongue probing
the small white flowers, followed by
a hummingbird, female, snaky tongue
preening pollen from her thin bill,
frightened off by an imperious
monarch nectaring lazily on
the pink blossoms of a neighboring plant.

3. National Defense

i.m.: Gogisgi/Carroll Arnett

A male ruby-throated hummingbird
drinks from a sapsucker well—holes drilled
in a precise series on the trunk
of a white birch. The hummingbird moves
its bill into each hole, except when
a National Guard jet roars over
at treetop level. Then the bird backs
out, watching the plane until it's gone.

BAY OF ISLANDS : Attacked by Oystercatchers

We'd gone on a sailboat with other tourists and moved out through islands
to the very limit of the bay. I finally saw two of the little blue penguins—
tiny footballs floating between waves—that I'd been hoping for. When we
were dropped at an uninhabited island for a couple of hours, most of my
companions sunned themselves on the beach, tried to swim in the water of
the South Pacific, still very cold on the first day of that antipodean summer,
or climbed the small hill to get the view. I walked through an easy valley to
the rocky shore on the opposite side and came out on a pair of oystercatchers
guarding a nest,

> bright neon bills
> > first, and then
> the red eye.

> They squawk,
> > flutter up at me.

> I stumble over black
> > volcanic rock.

THE GARDENER REMEMBERS

1.

The gardener sculpts the land
to help us remember the names
we've lost: wild ginger
and false Solomon's seal,
skunk cabbage and early buttercup.

The plants have outlasted
our indifference, their green lives
passing unnoticed among dunes
or woodland marshes, forgotten prairies
or alvar plains on northern islands.

The gardener remembers.

Children, coltish outdoors
after a long winter, might
gallop on the boardwalk
above Fleming Creek,
while an old man, stiff
in his knees, dozes
through the quiet breeze
that rustles cedar
and carries off
the rattle of woodpeckers.

But the gardener remembers
the Pitcher's thistle in the sand,
the cardinal flower above the creek.

2.

The gardener remembers to dig
down into soil, its mineral reek,
its slime, to coax up ephemerals
in spring, transplanted bloodroot, reminders
that metaphor is real and wonder
more than the condition of our loss.

3.

The gardener remembers
and those of us gathered
on the sculpted pathways
agree—whether we say it
or not—with the effort
to relearn these names.

*(On the Dedication of the Great Lakes Gardens
at Matthaei Botanical Gardens, April 14, 2013)*

MARGINALIA FOR A NATURAL HISTORY

for Jerry Dennis

1.

Passage to Eden
for Pete and Judith Becker

. . .

just to let you know that the true gate
to paradise is on an island
in a small lake, some far northern place
protected by seven months of cold
and ice, then four more of mosquitoes,
black flies, armies of them. Wolves and bear
if you're feeling brave. A few of us
know where it is, but we're not telling.

2.

In Leech Country

Undulant swimmer, like a blue gem
reflecting sunlight, the leech snaked up
below my canvas hightops, stretching
into air toward what warmth of mine
it sensed down there in northern water,
black, un-iced only five months a year.
My indolent, citified veins must
smell sweeter than blood of moose or pike.

3.

Running Down from the Hills

I limped too close to night and too far
into that dry south CA valley
and came out on a high sweaty trail
I didn't know. It took forever
on bad knees. Fog was blowing in cold
and I was hobbling down too slowly
when a mountain lion screamed somewhere
below me. I moved more quickly then.

4.

Not the Northwest Passage
    for Phil Myers

. . .

just the white-footed mouse, delicate
and doe-eyed, only twenty-five grams
of unrelenting passion pushing
north, a few feet each generation,
through duff on the forest floor, old logs
or tunnels under deep snow, always
north, attacking the necessary
and impenetrable wall of cold.

5.

At the Two Hearted
    for Ola Finke

. . .

just flitting around the eye's corner
but only seen when I learn the name—
ebony jewel-winged damselfly.
Luminous detail. Down low in shade
or catching quick moments of sunlight
on his green body, light reflecting
up through black gossamer wings, flashing
turquoise "into the clear, brown water."

6.

Reading Nabokov
    Will you ever forget it, I queried
    —That particular swift that went by?
    Fyodor Godunov-Cherdyntsev in *The Gift*

in the backyard, late-summer evening,
in my garden chair. A bird flies up
—a tufted titmouse, gray and urgent,
with intense, baleful eyes—and perches
above my left shoulder. When I turn
—so slowly, as gently as I can—
it jerks up and away, but its wing
unexpectedly brushes my cheek.

7.

While We Huddle Inside

crows in the volunteer hickory
sapling hunch against the wind and snow,
their backs the only crisp distinction
in the storm. They wait their turn to fly
down to our compost pile, then flutter
like awkward butterflies above the scraps
of lettuce and avocado peels,
before falling to their frozen meal.

8.

At the Living Crèche

A camel in the churchyard on State
walked around the fence toward our car
(This is true! It really did happen
late Christmas Eve after I picked up
Faith and Christine from Mass) and he bent
down to stick his head in the window.
Snow collected on his pelt. The steam
and stench of camel breath filled the air.

9.

Signs and Wonders

First flicker drumming on a dead ash
at the tail end of a harsh winter—
we've learned to cling to these simple things,
forgetting, for only a moment,
emerald-green ash borers killing
the trees, starlings chasing woodpeckers
from their holes, or the garlic mustard
that will sprout in profusion below.

10.

Once in this Life

at the Aransas Refuge, I watched
a whooping crane—at least five feet tall
with an eight-foot wingspan, black wing tips,
male, one of the last few hundred left
on earth—dip its head into the reeds.
I saw a drop of brackish water
form on his perfect bill, glisten once
in the sun, then fall back to the swamp.

11.

Spring Ephemerals and the Nature of Metaphor

The trout lily feels like metaphor—
its brown spotted leaves dominating
the forest floor for two or three weeks,
delicate yellow flowers drooping
and hard to find . . . then disappearing
one warm night when I forget to look—
but it's very real, underground now,
awaiting its chance to bloom next year.

12.

Above the Canopy
    for Steve Bertman

On a still morning, the hottest day
of the summer, not a single leaf
trembles, even at the very top
of the big-toothed aspen. Chorusing
thrush calls, syncopated by falling
harmonics—a veery there! again!
a robin! wood thrush to the north!
rise unbidden through the green below.

13.

Evidence
   for Ted Anderson

The evidence of things not seen is
in their song, like whippoorwills calling
from an old field above the river
at the last hint of twilight, pink sky
finally giving up to the dark,
echoing calls rising from bracken,
from birds seen only as quick shadows
whose song might move even the mountains.

14.

Canoeing at Dusk

I am a student in the landscapes
of light, alone on a quiet lake
as clouds fade from pink to gray, as green
shores darken into night. Watery
reflections, quickly shifting puddles
of purple half-light, play on the waves
I paddle through, first catching the last
hint of day, and then the waning moon.

KINGSTON PLAINS: The Ghost Forest

Gray stumps of white pines were almost charred into immortality by a fire so hot it burned off all the organic matter in the top several inches of soil. Little but lichen grew here for 130 years,

    and now,

        finally,

    a clump of small,

        ripe

blueberries.

SUMMER TEACHING

Driving the young scientists back
from a beaver dam, I listen to their talk

about life as information
encoded in letters
between spiraling strands of protein,
how we will soon
digitize our sequences
and the information that is us,
everything about us,
will never die.

I drive carefully on the back roads
and the freeway, hoping that whatever gods
left today haven't heard
or are off chasing beautiful children
who escape by turning into trees.

SCHUMANN, WHILE DRIVING

Swallows keep time
and cornfields become
scenes in Scandinavian films
I've never seen.

I drive through final credits
that follow an uncertain ending,
neither happy nor sad.

OUR CASTLE AND THE WILD DOGS

My daughter was sixteen when she learned
that we live in a dog-eat-dog world
and not the doggy-dog one she thought
she'd been living in. Just words, really,
but I'll admit feeling a bit pleased
that, without trying, we were able
to build such a castle, one to keep
off the wild dogs snarling in the dark.

TO FACE THE ORDINARY

There are moments when you step alone
from the forest into a long valley high
in the mountains, moments you will remember
when you sit for five minutes decades later,
catching your breath to face the ordinary world.
You look out and see moose or caribou
moving through the scrub. You stoop down
to tracks in the mud and spread your fingers
to measure the foot that walked here
(the paw is larger than your hand).
These moments, still filled with joy and fear
because an inch or two outside the track
are the clear, deep marks of a grizzly's claw.

ARGUMENT WITH EMILY: Amber Afternoons

Sunlight in the back room—
winter afternoons—
slants into corners
otherwise shaded—

the dark weeks—solstice
sun falling early—
low all day
across the yard—

but the back room—
these amber afternoons—
riots in its yellow light.

WINTER FINCHES

Christine chooses not to cut back
the stalks of our coneflowers
until spring, so the finches can pull
apart seeds all winter long.
They don't seem to appreciate that,
or the millet and thistle seeds,
the sunflower hearts and shelled peanuts
we buy for them. The gratitude's ours
when they descend every other day,
forty or fifty strong, a flurry
of light around the feeders.

ACOLYTES IN THE BIRD-WHILE

We have lingered in that space
granted by a woodpecker
before it disappears on the far side
of a dying elm. We have held
our collective breath as a warbler—
redstart, prothonotary, or golden-winged—
brushes across our shoulders. We have prayed
to avian gods we don't believe in
that piping plovers may avoid
windows, cats, and windmills,
will survive habitat loss,
climate change, and oil spills,
to allow us that one
immeasurable moment at sunset
when we count their glowing bills
among our fragile, vanishing gifts.

ACKNOWLEDGMENTS

Most of these poems first appeared, sometimes in very different forms, on the Academy of American Poets' poem-a-day website, and in the *Bear River Review, Big Scream, Border Crossing, Cheap Pop* (online), the *Collagist* (online), *Dunes Review, Escape Into Life* (online), *Fiddlehead* (Canada), *Hanging Loose, Hobart* (online), *Lansing On-line Journal,* the *MacGuffin, Mantis: A Journal of Poetry, Criticism & Translation,* the *Michigan Poet, Midwestern Gothic, New Ohio Review, Oleander, Pank, Poor Claudia, Structo* (UK), *Talking River,* and *Third Wednesday.*

"Drummond Island Fossils" first appeared in *The Way North: Collected Upper Peninsula New Works,* edited by Ron Riekki (Wayne State University Press, 2013).

"To Face the Ordinary" first appeared as a limited edition broadside published by Landmark Books/Squirrel Cane Press, Traverse City, MI, 2015.

Most of the eight-line poems or sequences of eight-line poems appeared, often in different constellations, in the chapbook *Marginalia for a Natural History* (Black Lawrence Press, 2011).

Several of these poems appeared in the chapbook *The Ancient Murrelet* (Alice Greene and Co., 2013).

Several of these poems appeared in the chapbook *Fidelities* (Alice Greene and Co., 2015).

The sequence "Mapping the River" appeared in a slightly different form in a multimedia presentation created for the Arts on Earth program at the University of Michigan. It was first performed at the Video Studio in the Duderstadt Center in November 2008.

"The Beginning" and "Green Light" were included in "Watershed," a short symphonic work by Evan Chambers commissioned by the Ann Arbor Symphony and first performed by that orchestra at the Michigan Theater in April 2009.

"Circle in the Wind" was commissioned by choreographer Jessica Fogel for her dance piece "In the Wind," which premiered on August 22, 2014, in an outdoor performance on the shores of Muskegon Lake.

"Castle, Nowhere" was commissioned by Patricia Clark and Virginia Jenkins for "Great Lakes: Image & Word," an exhibit at Grand Valley State University in Allendale, MI, that showcased collaborative work from January to April 2016. The poem was part of a piece executed in wood, paint, mixed media, and found objects by sculptor David Greenwood, titled "Starting Over (Searching for Castle Nowhere)."

I gratefully acknowledge the administrators, staff, faculty, students, and researchers at the University of Michigan Biological Station who have generously allowed me to eavesdrop on their conversations for more than ten years now.

A grant from the Center for Research on Learning and Teaching of the Provost's Office of the University of Michigan helped support part of this project.

The late A. L. "Pete" Becker first brought Emerson's discovery of "the bird-while" to my attention over twenty-five years ago.

In addition to the people mentioned in the various dedications, I need to thank my students, who haven't been shy about expressing their opinions about my poems or my obsessions, the booksellers who have sold my work, and the editors involved in the chapbook series, journals, and websites who have published parts of this book. I would like to give particular thanks to Charles Baxter, Clayton Eshleman, Tom Fricke, Steve Gillis, Laurence Goldstein, Lorna Goodison, Linda Gregerson, David James, A. Van Jordan, Laura Kasischke, Steve Leggett, Megan Levad, Thomas Lynch, Annie Martin, Khaled Mattawa, Ray McDaniel, the late Karl Pohrt, John Repp, Elizabeth Schmuhl, Marc Sheehan, Alison and David Swan, Richard Tillinghast, and Eric Torgersen, each of whom has been a necessary part of the conversation.

ABOUT THE AUTHOR

Portrait of Keith Taylor by Frank Born, 2014, oil on linen, 20 x 20 inches.

Keith Taylor teaches at the University of Michigan. He has published many books over the years: collections of poetry, a collection of very short stories, co-edited volumes of essays and fiction, and a volume of poetry translated from Modern Greek.

Tom Pohrt is a self-taught artist who has illustrated numerous books including *The New York Times* bestseller *Crow and Weasel* by Barry Lopez. He recently illustrated *Terrapin and Other Poems* by Wendell Berry and *Careless Rambles*, a selection of poems by John Clare. He lives in Ann Arbor, Michigan.